AIREDALE

TEN WALKS OF SIX MILES OR UNDER

Colin & Dorian Speakman

Dalesman

First published in 2011 by Dalesman
an imprint of
Country Publications Ltd
The Water Mill
Broughton Hall
Skipton
North Yorkshire BD23 3AG
www.dalesman.co.uk

Text © Colin Speakman & Dorian Speakman 2011
Maps © Gelder Design & Mapping 2011
Illustrations © Christine Isherwood 2011
Cover: the view from Malham Cove, by Derek Forss

ISBN 978-1-85568-284-9

Printed by Latitude Press Ltd.

PUBLISHER'S NOTE
....
The information given in this book has been provided in good faith and is intended
only as a general guide. Whilst all reasonable efforts have been made to ensure that
details were correct at the time of publication, the author and Country Publications
Ltd cannot accept any responsibility for inaccuracies. It is the responsibility of
individuals undertaking outdoor activities to approach the activity with caution and,
especially if inexperienced, to do so under appropriate supervision. The activity
described in this book is strenuous and individuals should ensure that they are
suitably fit before embarking upon it. They should carry the appropriate equipment
and maps, be properly clothed and have adequate footwear. They should also take
note of weather conditions and forecasts, and leave notice of their intended route
and estimated time of return.

Contents

Introduction

When you think about what makes Yorkshire seem like Yorkshire, you think about Airedale: a valley of towns and villages of solid millstone grit, canals, railways and the River Aire itself, slow and dark as it approaches the cities, but bright and sparkling in its upper reaches. Yet even in the towns, countryside is always close by. The main river is fed by numerous wooded narrow side-valleys, through which becks cascade from sheep-grazed moorland just above the rooftops of the towns, criss-crossed by patterns of stone walls that extend over the high peaty summits of the South Pennines.

Airedale is also the valley of Yorkshire's largest city, Leeds, with Bradford just to the south, and the towns of Shipley, Bingley, Keighley and Skipton on or close to the river as you travel north through the Aire Gap, one of the major natural passes through the Pennines. Beyond Skipton, Airedale is deeply rural. At Gargrave the valley transforms into Malhamdale, with some of the finest limestone country in England at your feet.

What makes Airedale special is this dramatic contrast between urban and rural. From the end of a street you make your way towards a wooded hillside or up onto the moor and, within a few minutes, dramatic views open out below you. Or you can discover that amazing green corridor shared by river, canal and railway, to find an older, pre-industrial valley of farms and woods, little changed by two centuries of industrial activity.

Airedale enjoys an excellent network of footpaths and good public transport. This selection of short walks extends from the source of the River Aire near Malham Tarn to the outskirts of Leeds. At the time of writing (spring 2011) all the walks are easily accessible from a parked car or by train and bus (for times, telephone 0870 6082608, or visit wwww.yorkshiretravel.net or www.dalesbus.org), with the exception of Walk 1 from Malham village which has a much less frequent bus service from Skipton. Within West Yorkshire, Day Rover tickets can save costs by both train and bus.

Most of Airedale away from the valley floor is real hill country. Paths are often steep, usually muddy and stiles require agility. Boots are essential most times of the year, and rainwear and emergency food and drink should always be carried. Have a good map — recommended are the Ordnance Survey maps 288, OL2 and OL21 as specified for each walk. Take all litter home with you, close gates (unless clearly propped open) and keep dogs on leads at all times — there are almost always sheep about.

The source of the Aire

Distance: 6 miles (10 km). Time: 2½ hours.
Start and finish: Malham National Park centre, grid ref 900627.
Parking: Malham village.
Terrain: footpaths and tracks; one climb of 600 feet (180 m).
Public transport: daily buses from Skipton, and Ilkley on summer Sundays.
Refreshments/facilities: cafés and two pubs in Malham, caravan serving
snacks by Malham Tarn on popular days; toilets in Malham.
Map: Ordnance Survey OL2 Southern & Western Dales.

*Malham is a popular spot due to spectacular landscape features such as
Malham Cove and Malham Tarn. This walk includes a visit to the cove and
its limestone pavement, Watlowes Dry Valley and the intriguing Water Sinks,
where the stream from the Tarn disappears completely, only to reappear at
Aire Head Springs (the source of the River Aire) below the village of
Malham. The walk returns via the less well-known paths over Ewe Moor.*

From the village centre, head up to the triangle road junction by the bridge
and bus stop. Take the road signed for the Tarn and Arncliffe. At the red
phone box turn right and go through the little gate into the woods, along the
path by Malham Beck. The path rejoins the road: follow it until the footpath
leads off for Malham Cove.

*Just before the turn-off, Town Head Barn contains a small National Trust
exhibition of local history and natural interest. The path passes fields on the
hillside rich in archaeological remains and ancient field systems.*

The well-maintained path leads to the cove. The path splits. Take the right
fork to the face of the cove, underneath which Malham Beck emerges.

*Malham Cove with its 200 foot (60 m) high sheer cliffs of limestone attracts
huge numbers of visitors, as well as peregrine falcons. At certain times of
the year the RSPB offers telescopes to watch these great birds of prey
nesting on the cliff. The formation of the cove is thought to have resulted
from a gigantic waterfall formed from meltwater from Ice Age glaciers; over
time the water has dissolved new paths deep under the limestone.*

Return to the left fork. The path climbs steadily up the side of the cove via
a series of stone steps. At the top, turn right and keep to the higher ground

5

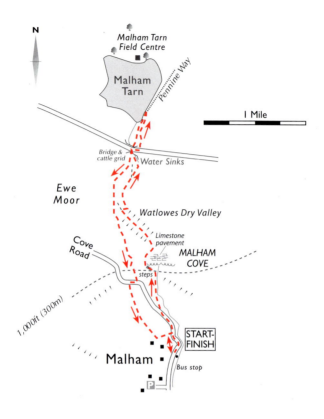

N

Malham Tarn
Field Centre

Malham
Tarn

Pennine Way

1 Mile

Bridge &
cattle grid

Water Sinks

Ewe
Moor

Watlowes Dry Valley

Limestone
pavement

MALHAM
COVE

Cove
Road

steps

1,000ft (300m)

START-
FINISH

Malham

Bus stop

P

on the left edge of the limestone pavement. Head left round the hillock to drop down to a gate at the bottom of the dry valley. Turn left to go through the gate (National Trust sign), taking the path up Watlowes Dry Valley to the stile. Turn right onto the path signed 'Malham Tarn'.

To the south is a grand view down Watlowes Dry Valley and in the distance the hills of Sharp Haw and Embsay Moor.

The path leads up to a fork. Bear right to go below an exposed limestone rockface, the path then levelling out as it approaches Water Sinks.

Water Sinks is where the stream from Malham Tarn flows underground for almost two miles (3 km) before reappearing below Malham village to merge with Malham Beck at Aire Head Springs, the source of the River Aire.

Follow the path up to the road. Turn right to cross the stream and go through the gate to the car park. Turn left here to go on the path straight ahead (Malham Tarn Field Centre is in view) towards the edge of Malham Tarn.

Malham Tarn is one of only two natural lakes in the Yorkshire Dales, incongruously located in limestone country where water invariably finds a way to disappear underground. Fed by the streams of Fountains Fell, the tarn itself was formed after the Ice Age, an ice-carved natural hollow dammed by clay, and is a site of great scientific interest — a highly suitable location for the Field Studies Council's Centre on the opposite shore. Surrounded by natural woodland, the landscape shows how different much of the Dales would be if protected from grazing.

From here take the path closer to the tarn edge to return back to the road and back as far as the signpost. Take the path signed 'Langscar Gate ½ mile', and at the next signpost turn left (signed 'Malham 1½ ml'). After about 100 yards the path enters a shallow dip. Don't take the more distinct path following the dip down, but instead continue in the same direction over stones. The grassy path soon descends down to the stiles above Watlowes. Take the first ladder-stile on the right and turn immediately left.

The curlew is a distinctive bird of the Malhamdale moors.

Continue in the same direction up to the ladder-stile with the National Trust sign. The next stile is straight ahead, as is the next stone stile. Now the path descends steadily, though it is less distinct at this stage. Keeping in the same direction, head for a gap-stile in the stone wall then towards the road ahead, below the double bend sign. The path emerges onto the road.

Turn right to climb a short distance up to the sharp corner. Go down the grassy path (signed 'Malham 1') that leads to an enclosed lane. This grassy lane becomes stony, passing a water treatment building, descending steadily towards Malham village. At the T-junction turn left. Take the next right, a stony path between trees. Go straight down into the village, rejoining the tarn road. Turn right for the village centre.

Airton & Bell Busk

Distance: 4½ miles (7 km). **Time:** 2 hours.
Start: Airton village green crossroads, grid ref 903593.
Parking: Airton, by village green or on roadside; limited parking in laybys
by river bridge on Hetton road.
Terrain: field paths and tracks; one short climb.
Refreshments/facilities: Town Head Farm shop and café 250 yards north of
village on Malham road; no toilets in village.
Public transport: Bus 210/211 weekdays (not Tues/Thurs), summer Sundays
Dalesbus 883/4 and some winter Sundays.
Map: Ordnance Survey Explorer OL2.

A walk to explore a section of Pennine Way and less frequented paths in the rolling countryside of Malhamdale. Airton, like Saltaire, takes its name from its river but is a far older settlement, mentioned in Domesday Book. The village has some fine old houses and a Quaker Meeting House built by William Ellis, a local linen weaver, in 1697.

From the crossroads, walk down the lane towards Calton to the mill and bridge.

Airton Mill, now residential apartments, began life as a water-powered corn mill then converted to cotton spinning in the late eighteenth century, and even enjoyed a short spell as an engineering works in the twentieth century.

Cross the bridge to join the Pennine Way at a stile (right), signed 'Gargrave 4 miles'. Follow a pretty section of river through a narrow pasture. Where the river bends right, the Pennine Way keeps straight ahead to a stone step-stile (904586). Bear left towards the river over two stiles to follow the wall by Newfield Laithe. Over the next stile, bear right towards Newfield Bridge.

Cross the bridge. Take the Pennine Way, left over a wooden stile and along a narrow path between wood and river. Take the pedestrian gate, right, into the woods, walking above a retaining wall then into a field. Head for the footbridge straight ahead. Go left along a narrow field alongside the road into Eshton Moor, a large open pasture. The Pennine Way heads straight ahead uphill to join a narrow but distinct path, a wood over a disused quarry to your left. Ascend the brow of the hill to where, half-right, is a tall finger-post. This marks a bridleway to a gate through the wall, right (914571).

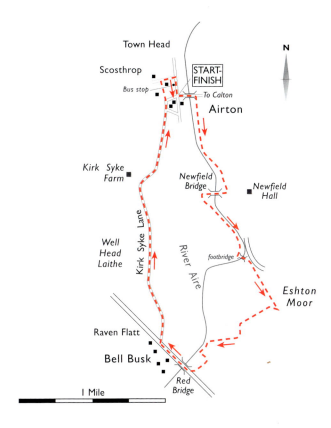

Town Head

Scosthrop

START-FINISH

Bus stop

To Calton

Airton

N

Kirk Syke Farm

Newfield Bridge

Newfield Hall

Kirk Syke Lane

Well Head Laithe

River Aire

footbridge

Eshton Moor

Raven Flatt

Bell Busk

Red Bridge

I Mile

Go through the gate, then bear half-right climbing up the field, with the trig station on Haw Crag to your left (superb views of Malhamdale). As a wall comes into view, take the second gap in the wall, right, and bear left to locate a grass track to a gate. Turn right down the wallside by a meadow, passing a barn and gate to rejoin little River Aire. Turn left towards a small weir, before which you turn left through a metal gate through a small stable yard, then right along the farm track to its junction with Mark House Lane. Turn right, then over a fine old river bridge on this pre-turnpike highway to join the metalled road. Keep ahead at the junction with the Airton road over Red Bridge to join the lane through Bell Busk.

Bell Busk almost certainly takes it name from a long-vanished medieval roadside tavern on the old Leeds-Kendal road. A 'busk' or bush was an inn sign and the bell would be the inn name. Tudor House, visible through trees on the left, is now a country house hotel but was formerly Bell Busk Railway Station, once busy with day trippers who alighted at 'Bell Busk for Malham' from trains on the Leeds-Morecambe or Settle-Carlisle railways.

Walk past the old station (now hotel) entrance, to take the bridleway right, just before the house known as Raven Flatt (903566). This begins as an unsurfaced track past rickety farm buildings to a bridge where it forks left at a barn (waymarked). Follow the fence along the next field. At the field end, the bridleway goes through the wooden gate and along the far side of the field.

This is Kirk Syke Lane, the main route in Edwardian times on foot and waggonette from Bell Busk Station to Malham.

At the next gate the ancient, sunken nature of the way becomes more evident, as it winds past old hedges and the buildings of Well Head Laithe, climbing gently up the slopes of Colgarth Hill.

You eventually reach a little ford with a little footbridge alongside. This is Kirk Syke ('syke' means small stream). Pass the entrance to Kirk Syke Farm where the way broadens to a farm road, before joining the back lane to Airton. At the crossroads (901591) turn right then first left by Lambert House.

The dipper favours fast-flowing stretches of water in upland areas.

Go straight ahead and then slightly right at Gategarth, along a green way descending behind Airton to emerge in the hamlet of Scosthrop.

The name Scosthrop is suggestive of Norse settlers keeping a friendly but respectable distance from their Anglian neighbours in Airton.

Turn right here past the two small village greens to the main road, then right for bus stop and parked cars, or left to Town Head Farm for refreshments.

Gargrave & the Pennine Way

Distance: **5 miles (8 km)**. Time: **2½ hours.**
Start: **Gargrave, road junction by Dalesman Café, grid ref 932542.**
Parking: **free car parks by crossroads or in West Street.**
Terrain: **canal towpath and field paths; one gentle climb.**
Refreshments/facilities: **café, shops and pubs in Gargrave; toilets by bus stop.**
Public transport: **all Leeds-Skipton-Morecambe and some Settle-Carlisle
trains call at Gargrave; Bus 580 from Skipton (regular service), DalesBus
Cravenlink 883/4 (Sundays Easter–October, limited winter service).**
Map: **Ordnance Survey Explorer OL2.**

*This walk starts and finishes at the picturesque coaching village of
Gargrave, on the former Keighley-Kendal turnpike road (now the A65). It
combines a fascinating stretch of the towpath of the Leeds-Liverpool Canal,
with a less well-known section of the Pennine Way, crossing the beautiful
area of Craven drumlins that link the South Pennines and Yorkshire Dales.*

From the Dalesman Café, walk along West Street, following the lane as it
winds to the left to the bridge over the Leeds-Liverpool Canal. Turn left onto
the canal towpath.

*The 127 mile (203 km) Leeds-Liverpool Canal was the first waterway to
cross the Pennines, and is still a magnificent feat of canal engineering, with
its series of locks and aqueducts as it twists its way west of Gargrave
through the Aire Gap. It was opened as far as Gargrave from Leeds by 1780
to carry lead, zinc ore, and limestone from the Yorkshire Dales to industrial
West Yorkshire. It was extended to the Lancashire border by the 1790s, but
because of lack of money the final sections through to Wigan to connect with
the canal from Liverpool were not completed until 1816.*

Follow the towpath as it leads alongside the woods of Gargave Park, going
under the A65 by the Anchor Inn and Anchor Locks, passing Scarland Lock
before turning southwards heading for two railway bridges, the longer and
more ornate crossing the River Aire, the shorter one the canal. The canal is
then carried over the remarkable short aqueduct over the little River Aire.

*Surprisingly, this part of the river hardly has its own valley or dale, but
squeezes and twists between the high green hillocks or drumlins, mounds of
glacial waste, as it flows southwards from Malhamdale.*

11

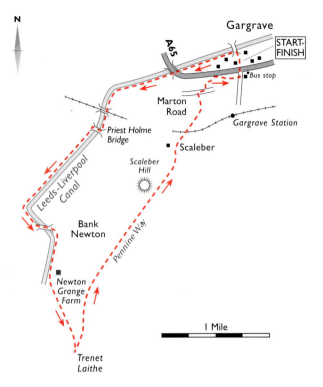

At Priest Holme Bridge (917537) the towpath joins the lane. Go onto and over the bridge, then turn left and follow the lane for some 400 yards. Rejoin the canal side again along the towpath by Newton Bank Moorings.

You follow a series of six locks each with their holding ponds which now serve as small marinas. You soon reach the top lock, Lock 41, at Newton Head. Though this isn't quite the summit of the canal, water supplies were always a problem and in the 1890s an aqueduct was constructed to supply water from a new reservoir at Winterburn, five miles (8 km) to the north.

Where the next bridge, Newton Changeline (912528), crosses the canal — note the unusual surviving roller to protect towing ropes — the towpath twists up and over the bridge. Cross, now following the lane alongside the canal. Do not go through the little gate back onto the towpath, but continue along the lane past Newton Grange Farm. The lane becomes a stony track and climbs gently up the hillside past Great Meadow Plantation.

Note the high level of the canal just visible in the hillside to the left as it follows a series of complex meanders, carefully hugging the contours to save yet more expensive locks and water — one of the finest examples in the UK of a late eighteenth-century contour canal.

The track descends to a shallow valley formed by a stream, Nuttleber Dyke (915517). Look for a stile just before the track bends left. This leads onto the Pennine Way. Notice the little acorn National Trail waymark.

Your route is now over a series of wide pastures, heading north-north-west. Descend to a shallow valley north of Trenet Laithe, across two stiles and a small footbridge. Go due north following a fence and stretch of woodland, keeping to the right of a short stretch of crossing fence. Head to the next stile and the end of a fence then, past a wood, to the wide gate ahead (917523).

Mallards are a common sight along the stretches of the Leeds-Liverpool Canal covered by the walks in this book.

Keep straight ahead, heading due north-eastwards, over stiles, all waymarked, crossing to the other side of the fence as you gently climb the shallow saddle between Scaleber and Moorber Hill, two very characteristic drumlins. Reach a crossing of paths by a large signpost.

This is a magnificent viewpoint across the Aire Gap, with views northwards into Malhamdale and across to Barden Moor with Cracoe War Memorial a notable landmark.

Keep straight ahead on the Pennine Way as you reach the track to Scaleber Farm, heading for the pedestrian gate straight ahead. This leads to the stony track known as Mosber Lane. Descend the track, going across the railway bridge. Ignore the Pennine Way bearing off right to keep ahead to Marton Road on the edge of Gargrave. Turn right for 100 yards, left along Walton Avenue then the first gap to the right, past the 'No vehicles' sign, which leads to Gargrave's pretty riverside village green. Keep straight ahead past the small village pond to Gargrave Bridge. Gargrave Railway Station is to the right, bus stops, café and car parks to the left.

13

Skipton to Cononley

Distance: 5 miles (8 km). Time: 2½ – 3 hours.
Start: Skipton, Sir Matthew Wilson statue, opposite town hall, High Street,
grid ref 990518. Finish: Cononley.
Parking: Skipton town centre, to return by train.
Terrain: one climb of 200 yards; footpaths and tracks.
Refreshments/facilities: numerous cafés, shops and pubs in Skipton, pubs
in Carleton and Cononley; toilets in Skipton car park.
Public transport: Skipton has frequent trains and buses; Cononley has
frequent trains and buses back to Skipton.
Map: Ordnance Survey OL21 South Pennines.

This walk leads out of Skipton to cross Airedale over to the village of Carleton up the imposing hillside of Carleton Moor, with fine views of the Yorkshire Dales; once over the ridge the view changes towards lower Airedale and Lothersdale. The walk finishes in the quiet village of Cononley, which belies its tranquil air by having good transport links.

Skipton has a strategic location in the Aire Gap, the pass through the Pennines exploited by road, canal and railway. Although it has had its fair share of industry (in Skipton's case, cotton), Skipton remains a historic market town with a castle, on the edge of the Yorkshire Dales.

From the statue head down High Street and Sheep Street before turning right under the archway opposite Edinburgh Woollen Mill. Keep ahead past the stone kiosk along the lane to the right, turning left onto Coach Street to meet Belmont Street. Turn right over Belmont Bridge then right again along the Leeds-Liverpool Canal towpath. Follow the towpath to the second swing bridge before turning left to the main road opposite the station. (If you arrive by train you can join the route here.)

Take the road sharp right towards Carleton, up to and over the bridge to take the next turn right, Engine Shed Lane. Follow this road to the end, passing the small industrial estate. Take the next left, a tarmac lane, and go through the gate (stile on left side) to go under the Skipton bypass through a tunnel.

Keep straight ahead to follow the track on the right which crosses a drain before a stone stile, then head for the bridge crossing the River Aire. Go over the bridge. Take the path leading off left away from the next stile.

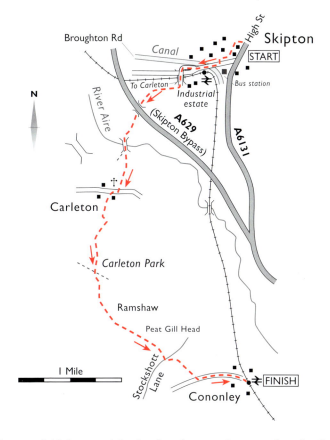

In the next field, keep straight ahead to the gate, then over the stile. Go through a wrought-iron gate and up to the churchyard, heading for the gate just to the left. Turn right at the junction. In front of the church turn left into Carleton village centre.

Turn right, following the road signed for Colne. Past the converted mill take the footpath leading from the left side of the road, just before the bridge. Go up through the trees, then up the steps straight ahead, over the drive and straight ahead again. Follow the path up the hill. Where the wall juts out, continue up the hill, following the remains of a wall, which is little more than a raised heap of stones. Turn left where the line of another old wall appears on the ground, heading for the lower of two gates (971492).

Go through the gate to join the narrow road. Head uphill for about 275 yards before turning left onto a track. Take the small gate on the right. Go along the left edge of the field, and then over a stile, which is awkward on the other side. Head up the slope towards the gate. Bend towards the left side of the field, heading for a group of trees behind the wall, before following the wall to the corner of the field and a gate. In front is Carleton Park Farm. Head over the stream to the track by the side of the farm. Go through the gate marked with a waymark arrow. Follow the wall along the edge of the farm. By a mini sheep pen, head for a metal gate ahead (969481) roughly in the direction of 1 o'clock. Go through the gate and up a faint track on the right side of the moorland field.

Look out for the yellowhammer in the open country along this walk.

As you ascend, increasingly fine views over Airedale open out, looking further towards Wharfedale and Fountains Fell.

The track leads to the top of the ridge known as Ramshaw, where another wider path is crossed. Continue straight ahead on a grassy path leading down the other side of the ridge. Look for the yellow waymarks on the wall, and the next stile, which is a gap in the wall ahead. Follow the wall down along the side of the field.

Through a narrow gap-stile, passing a Peat Gill Farm to the left, the path continues with a waymark post ahead indicating the path down a shallow dip, before curving up to Moor Top farm on the left, which has a wind turbine in a neighbouring field. Head up to a stile in the corner of the field by the farm (977474).

Join the track and turn right, heading over the cattle grid. Follow the track down to Stockshott Lane. Cross over to take the footpath straight ahead. At the next stile turn left as the sign indicates, following the drystone wall. The path leads down the fieldside to a lane. Turn left down to Cononley.

Turn right at the junction to follow the road down through the village. Bus stops are by the post office in the village centre. Continue along the road to Cononley station, just past the level crossing.

Wainman's Pinnacle & Lund's Tower

Distance: 4½ miles (7 km). Time: 2½ – 3 hours.
Start and finish: Cowling, Fold Lane, grid ref 973431.
Parking: limited to side streets in Cowling.
Terrain: Footpaths; total ascent 500 feet (200 m).
Public transport: Bus 25 between Keighley and Burnley, using the bus
stops by the traffic lights in the centre of Cowling.
Refreshments/facilities: café, pub and chip shop in Cowling.
Map: Ordnance Survey OL21 South Pennines.

This walk offers a spectacular contrast in a short distance. Early stages are dominated by a long, steep ridge with one of the best viewpoints in the South Pennines, returning along field and woodland paths. Cowling is Saxon in origin, and it is thought that the name is derived from 'Coll's tribe'. Once the Keighley-Colne turnpike road was constructed, the mills followed. Now Cowling is a commuter village for towns in Lancashire and West Yorkshire.

From the traffic lights, head down the main street and turn left up Fold Lane. Where the road narrows, a footpath sign indicates the way straight ahead, the road becoming a single-track lane. Walk up between farm buildings and through the gate. Note the waymark by the next gate, and bend right to climb the hill. Take the first footpath left in front of the trees, going up the hillside to a stone stile. Go through the wooden gate above, then turn right to take the path following the wall up the ridge. Note the waymark on the post.

On clear days there are panoramic views west towards Pendle Hill in Lancashire, south across the South Pennines, and north towards Simons Seat and Buckden Pike in Wharfedale, and Pen-y-ghent in Ribblesdale.

Continue straight ahead just to the left of the barn, over a stile following the tracks leading towards Wainman's Pinnacle. At the bend in the track, peel off left onto a grassy track; this leads up to Wainman's Pinnacle.

Wainman's Pinnacle is a tall triangular tower, built by the Wainman family to commemorate the defeat of Napoleon in 1815. It was badly damaged by lightning over later years, so in 1900 it was demolished and rebuilt.

Next head for the gate ahead and along the ridge path towards Lund's Tower. By a stone seat the path meets a concrete path by a small kissing-gate.

17

At the end of the ridge is Lund's Tower, built by James Lund of Malsis Hall. It is possible to climb up its winding staircase, but a torch is advisable. The two towers are known locally as the Salt and Pepper Pots.

From the tower, head down back to the gate, but turn sharp right down the concrete steps and winding path to the minor road below. Turn left on to the road and follow it down for about 350 yards. At the double footpath sign on the right, take the path which turns sharp left to go down to the lower gate. Head down the enclosed path, over two stone stiles, then take the stile on the left to head towards Crag End Farm. Crossing the field, keep the farm in view as you descend, then join the track near the farm entrance. Turn right to follow the track down to the main road.

Cross the A6068 and turn left as far as New Hall Farm. Go down the drive to a cobbled area, looking for the white gate at the end of the row of houses (983442). The path now goes half-left across the garden lawn to a stone stile. The path turns left for 10 yards, then crosses the grown-out remnants of a hedge on the left. Turn right and follow the hedge through a narrow field, heading for the farm buildings. Go through the wide farm gate on the left just before the farm buildings and walk through the farmyard, down the access track to join the lane near Lane Ends.

Turn right towards Lane Ends, but at the road corner (980443) cross the footbridge left over the river. Go up the steps ahead and turn right to follow the path upstream for about half a mile, passing the site of Ridge Mill Bridge, at the time of writing due to be rebuilt after storm damage occurred in 2008.

Cross Gill Beck over the sturdy wooden bridge (972438). Turn left, following the path as it swings right to go upstream again, before ascending the slope on the left. Head for the stile, then follow the edge of the field until the next stile in front of the farm shed.

Turn left onto the track, going over the gap-stile by the gate, and follow the track (Cinder Hill Lane) down through the wood to join a stone-flagged path. Turn right to cross over the footbridge and follow the path which leads to a track into Cowling, turning right for the village centre.

Doubler Stones

Distance: 6 miles (9.5 km). Time: 3 hours.
Start: Steeton Memorial Gardens, opposite parish church, grid ref 042464.
Parking: Pay and display car park by Memorial Gardens.
Terrain: canal towpath, quiet tracks and field paths; some strenuous
sections; total climb 900 feet (275 m).
Refreshments/facilities: cafés, shops and inns; toilets opposite Gardens.
Public transport: Keighley-Ilkley Bus 762/765 (if coming from Keighley
alight at Elliot Street close to canal bridge); Steeton & Silsden Station
(Airedale Line) is 1 mile away, Bus 762/765 passes the station.
Map: Ordnance Survey Explorer OL21.

*This walk is quintessential Airedale: a mixture of industrial heritage,
gritstone buildings, farmland, wooded gills and open moorland.*

Walk along Kirkgate to the canal bridge. Cross, taking the steps left alongside Bridge Inn to the towpath. Follow the towpath for just over a mile to
Holden Bridge (052450). Cross and follow the grassy track leading past Howden
Grange Farm to the lane. Turn right. Climb steeply up the lane to the hairpin.
A bridleway left (signed) leads from the corner by gate and stile. Follow the
sandy track. At a fork where the track leads down to a cottage, take the
grassy path right. After 100 yards take the path that bears left at a waymark
post (062453). This narrow path descends into a gill above Holden Beck.

Follow the path with care, eventually crossing a beck by a waterfall and to
a wooden stile in the top wall corner. Rejoin the bridleway at a gate leading
to a ford and footbridge at the gill head below an overhead pipeline.

Cross to join the green track which bears left towards a wall. Ignore the stile
ahead but bear right up the wall side. The wall eventually curves to the right
and reaches a farm track and stile (067458). Turn left to a metal gate.
Beyond it, turn left around the outside of the buildings to reach a crossing
of gravel tracks. Turn right here and right again past the farmhouse, but left
at the next junction of tracks to pass a farm cottage heading towards the tall
stone pillars of Far Ghyll Grange. Follow the track to the left. At the next
junction (068460) turn sharp left up an enclosed green way into open
pasture. Follow the wall on the left to reach a concrete farm track (signed).
Turn sharp right here, through the gate and past the bungalow. After about
50 yards turn right onto the (faint) path towards Doubler Stones (073466).

19

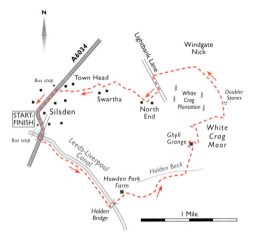

These two wind-carved gritstone crags at the edge of Rombalds Moor are a distinctive local landmark, with spectacular views down into central Airedale and to the high moors of the South Pennines above Haworth Moor.

The path below Doubler Stones heads to a small pedestrian gate leading to a narrow path across to Addingham High Moor. Follow the path through the heather past shooting butts to a stone gap-stile and the crest of the hillside. (This is Windgate Nick, and on an ancient packhorse route.) Turn left towards the plantation, following the path as it descends and curves right to follow the wall down to Nab End and Lightbank Lane (062471).

Turn left for about 300 yards to where a signed footpath right indicates the path alongside two fields before curving right down towards North End. The path goes through the left of two pedestrian gates, past the garden and along the drive. Immediately past the house, leave the drive to descend a grass slope to the gap-stile in the wall below right (058467). Keep the same direction through the next stile ahead, but in the big pasture below, head for a point some 50 yards to the south of the wooden electricity pole into a hollow. On the left, by a wall, a waymark indicates the path which bridges the beck to a stile alongside a gate. Follow the path up the slope to the gate and stile in the farm track ahead. Turn right to a stile which leads into a path parallel to the track. Turn sharp left here through metal gates to join the track past High Swartha Farm. Keep ahead to the lane (053469).

Your path (waymarked 'Millennium Way') is straight ahead through the pedestrian gate. Follow the waymark posts and clear path, which bears left alongside a wall to join an enclosed path. Where this bends sharp left, take the waymarked path straight ahead. Descend alongside a hedge through two fields before reaching another enclosed path by allotments. Turn right to follow the path which joins the Addingham road at Silsden Town Head. Turn left for the town centre, or the bus stop to Ilkley is opposite.

St Ives & Druids' Altar

Distance: 4½ miles (7 km). Time: 2½ hours.
Start and Finish: Bingley Railway Station, grid ref 108392.
Parking: Bingley town centre.
Terrain: footpaths and tracks; one climb of 200 yards.
Public transport: Bingley has half-hourly trains from Leeds and Bradford;
buses from Bradford (662), Leeds (760), Keighley (662, 760).
Refreshments/ facilities: cafés and pubs in Bingley, café in St Ives Estate;
toilets in Bingley market place.
Map: Ordnance Survey Explorer 288 Bradford & Huddersfield.

A walk from the banks of the River Aire up to Druids' Altar, a fine Airedale viewpoint; from here the route goes over the hillside to the parkland of St Ives and the secluded valley of Harden Beck before returning over the river and through Bingley's Myrtle Park to the town centre.

Bingley is a pleasant former milltown which has kept its character, despite being set in the busier built up part of Airedale, and is famous for the late eighteenth-century Five Rise Locks on the Leeds-Liverpool Canal.

From the station, turn left and cross the car park in front of the entrance heading towards Foundry Hill. Go up the short cobbled passageway to the main street crossing at the pelican crossing. Head to the right of the market place, following the Riverside Walk sign directing you down Queen Street towards the metal arch. Take the sloping path to the right down to the riverside. Follow the path ahead along the River Aire. The path then snakes past some houses before emerging at a road.

Turn left to cross over the river bridge. At the corner, opposite the Brown Cow pub, take the path with the steps up the hill. Where it meets a track, turn right to continue up the hill, a steady climb through the woods and fields.

Just as the track levels out, turn right onto a grassy path passing under the power lines. The path goes through a mixture of bracken and heather, and reaches the ridge edge. Continue along the ridge, passing the large gritstone crags of Druids' Altar, overlooking the valley below.

The view from Druids' Altar is spectacular, with the upland of Rombalds Moor opposite, and the edges of Keighley and Bingley below.

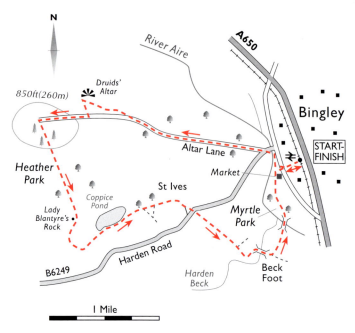

N

River Aire

A650

Druids' Altar

850ft(260m)

Bingley

Altar Lane

START-FINISH

Heather Park

Market

St Ives

Myrtle Park

Coppice Pond

Lady Blantyre's Rock

Harden Road

Beck Foot

B6249

Harden Beck

1 Mile

Follow the path in the same direction up to where it crosses a tarmac lane. Turn left. The tarmac soon finishes, and the lane leads back to Altar Lane.

At the junction, turn right through the gate with the 'No Cars' sign. Follow the lane up the last gentle part of the climb. At the hilltop, turn left through the kissing-gate and take the path straight ahead. Follow this down, ignoring the tracks bearing off left and right. The path takes a gentle descent through mixed woodland of conifer and birch, and an expanse of heather moor which has some recolonisation by trees and rhododendron bushes.

Flowers of the sycamore.

At Lady Blantyre's Rock is a memorial to the Dowager Lady Blantyre, who died in 1875. She was the mother-in-law of the squire of St Ives, William Busfeild Ferrand, Member of Parliament at various times for Knaresborough and Devonport. The memorial is a tribute to a place that she frequented to enjoy the view and the tranquillity for reading.

22

The path passes the memorial to Lady Blantyre, and descends down through increasingly mature woodland. Passing a cleared area, the track runs along the side of Coppice Pond. Exit the parkland by the gates and cross over the road to take the path opposite.

St Ives Estate park, which lies to the left, has a rich natural heritage. It is home to five species of bat, and numerous bird species such as jays, woodpeckers, tits and finches. It has a playground for children as well as a bird hide in the woods by Coppice Pond. The estate's history stretches from the twelfth century when it was owned by Cistercian monks until 1540, whereupon it passed into the hands of the Ferrand family. In 1928 the family sold the estate to Bingley Urban District Council, superseded by Bradford Metropolitan District Council, which runs the estate for public recreation. Nearby is the Sports Turf Research Institute, which developed and grew the turf used in the World Cup in South Africa in 2010.

Go straight ahead at the footpath junction, passing a stone wall then picnic tables. Ignore the turn-offs as you approach a low wall on the left. The path rounds the edge of a mansion house, before descending further to a road.

Long-tailed tits are residents of woodland like that on the St Ives Estate.

Along the roadside is a small plaque marking the stump of the Ferrands Oak which was used for the new transept of York Minster. The original had been damaged by fire in 1984.

Follow the road down for 400 yards, passing the old lodge and round a hairpin bend; 20 yards past the car park exit, take the path surrounded by wooden bollards. At the fork take the right-hand path which descends to a road.

Cross this to go down Beckfoot Lane. Follow the lane down to the houses, whereupon it bends left and enters some woodland. Cross over the hump-backed bridge. Just past the allotments, take the next path left. Cross over the River Aire heading into Myrtle Park up the slope. Keep to the left of the playground, passing the memorial, to exit at the back of the park. Head down the road to emerge at the far side of Bingley market place.

Shipley Glen & Hirst Wood

Distance: 4 miles (7 km). Time: 2 hours.
Start: Saltaire, railway bridge above station, grid ref 139380.
Parking: Free car park behind Salts Mill, pay and display car parks in
Victoria Road and Exhibition Road.
Terrain: mainly woodland paths and tracks.
Refreshment/facilities: cafés and shops in Saltaire, pub and café in Shipley
Glen; toilets in Victoria Road car park.
Public transport: all Airedale line Leeds/Bradford–Skipton trains stop at
Saltaire; Bus 662 (frequent) from Bradford, Bus 760 from Leeds.
Map: Ordnance Survey Explorer 288.

This walk can be combined with a visit to the remarkable UNESCO World
Heritage industrial village of Saltaire and celebrated Salts Mill gallery. The
route passes the site of the former Victorian pleasure grounds of Shipley
Glen, taking in some interesting features of the Leeds-Liverpool Canal and
areas of semi-natural Pennine oak woodland, including Hirst Wood.

From the railway bridge, head down Victoria Road over the canal bridge.
Bear left to the canal towpath and into the entrance to Roberts Park.

Roberts Park was opened in 1871 to the designs of William Gay (1814-93)
for Sir Titus Salt as part of the model industrial town of Saltaire for the
health and wellbeing of the town's workers and families. Initially known as
the People's Park, it was finally donated to the city of Bradford by James
Roberts, manager of Salts Mill. Its bandstand and other fine public
buildings have been superbly restored.

Keep straight ahead on the main path, curving by the park fence to just past
a stone shelter. On the right the rear entrance from the park leads into High
Coach Road near Salt Grammar School. Turn right here, crossing the road
at the pedestrian crossing. Passing the bus turning circle, follow the tall
hedge to reach the path (left), signed to leading to Shipley Glen tramway.

Shipley Glen Tramway is Britain's oldest working cable tramway, built in
1895, and still operating most weekends and holiday times. Its 1 foot 8 inch
(508 mm) gauge and brightly coloured track cars make a colourful feature.
It once brought people up to Shipley Glen Pleasure Grounds, a Victorian
funfair which survived into the early years of the present century.

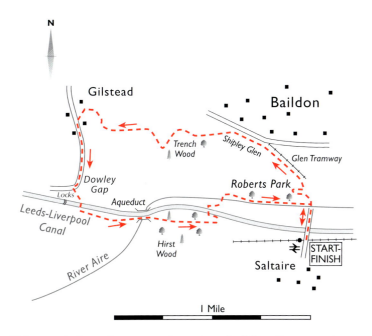

N

Gilstead

Baildon

Trench Wood

Shipley Glen

Glen Tramway

Dowley Gap

Locks

Roberts Park

Aqueduct

Leeds-Liverpool Canal

River Aire

Hirst Wood

START-FINISH

Saltaire

1 Mile

If the tram isn't running, or you choose to walk, follow the narrow tarmac path alongside, up to the summit station, keeping ahead into Prod Lane. Keep ahead passing the site of the old funfair on your left until you reach the open common land of Baildon Moor at the top of the Glen (133388) by Old Glen House pub.

Follow the track left past the pub, just below the edge of the moor. Keep straight ahead as it descends along the wooded side of Shipley Glen to join a bridleway which descends to the floor of the Glen below the moor edge. As you reach a small millpond ahead, turn left along the path between stone walls, with a cobbled central stretch, climbing steeply up the glen side. Head up the hillside past Delph Wood. Keep left along the track enclosed between stone walls at the next junction (126388), heading up towards Gilstead. The enclosed track, known as Sparable Lane, bears sharply right, curving round the back of a house and garden before eventually emerging in Primrose Lane at the edge of Gilstead.

Turn left here, crossing to the pavement to avoid the traffic, and descend the steep hillside for about 600 yards. Where Primrose Lane turns right, look for a narrow path on the left which leads to a bridge over the canal close to

Dowley Gap locks on the Leeds-Liverpool Canal. Follow the track to the left, past old farm buildings and the water treatment works, to reach the impressive Dowley Gap Aqueduct carrying the canal over the River Aire.

You now enter Hirst Wood, an area of beautiful, semi-natural woodland, mainly oak and birch. The wood is also noted for wild flowers, especially bluebells in spring; and for its birdlife, including woodpecker, jay, nuthatch, treecreeper, long-tailed tit and the occasional owl.

There is a choice of paths in the woodland, but the second track left is especially attractive, leading over the spine of the low hill covered by lovely

Wood anemone and celandine can be found in wooded areas.

oak woods. Keep straight ahead to the end of the wood. Bear left on the main paths that converge close to Hirst Wood locks and swing bridge over the canal.

You can walk back by the Leeds-Liverpool Canal towpath, but as this is usually busy with cyclists, for a quieter walk turn right for some 20 yards to where on the left a narrow stone gap-stile leads down to the footbridge over the River Aire. Cross, and turn right along the banks of the River Aire alongside open grassland. Keep ahead to the gate which leads into Roberts Park by the cricket ground. Follow the path past the cricket ground into the main part of the park. Turn right at the junction of paths where you started, past the Boathouse Inn and back across the bridges over river and canal to the centre of Saltaire.

Esholt village & Spring Wood

Distance: 4 miles (6.5 km). Time: 2 hours.
Start: Baildon Railway Station, grid ref 163393. Finish: Guiseley.
Parking: Shipley or Guiseley (and use train); limited parking in Baildon.
Terrain: field paths; some quiet road walking; about 300 feet of ascent.
Refreshments/facilities: pubs and cafés in Esholt and Guiseley.
Public transport: Wharfedale Line train service from Bradford and Shipley
to Baildon, and from Guiseley to Bradford, Baildon, Shipley and Leeds.
Map: Ordnance Survey Explorer 288 Bradford & Huddersfield.

This easy station to station walk follows the banks of the River Aire to the village of Esholt, made famous by Yorkshire Television's Emmerdale Farm. *From there the walk follows woodland paths through unspoiled Spring Wood, and climbs gradually to the busy township of Guiseley. A route through quiet back streets leads into the town centre and the railway station.*

The first record of Baildon dates from AD 835, when it was part of an area around Otley gifted to the Archbishop of York. It is thought that Baildon developed from a scattering of farmsteads and cottages which were centred around the feudal manor. Starting in the sixteenth century, manufacturing of cloth transformed from a cottage-based industry to workshops and mills. In addition, coal was mined and stone quarried around Baildon Moor. Baildon's growth accelerated during the Industrial Revolution and with the coming of the railways, and the town has since developed as a residential area serving both Bradford and Leeds.

From Baildon Station, take the exit with the steps leading up the side of the bridge. Go over the bridge then turn left. Go down the steps and follow the path which becomes a track before emerging at a road. Turn right. Follow the road down to the junction with Otley Road and cross the road using the traffic island on the right. Head back to go down Buck Lane.

Where the track forks, take the right fork to pass terraced houses. Just before the bridge, turn left to take the riverside path along the River Aire. The path emerges at a gap in the metal fence at a field corner.

Turn right along Esholt Lane into Esholt. Past the cricket ground, turn left up the footpath by the allotments. Turn right to rejoin Esholt Lane. Follow this into the village centre, past the post office and Woolpack Inn.

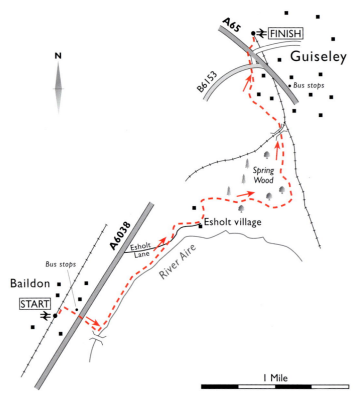

For many years the popular Yorkshire Television soap opera Emmerdale Farm *(now just* Emmerdale*) was filmed on location at Esholt, until a specially constructed 'replica' film set based on the buildings of Esholt was established at Harewood in 1997. Less well known is the nearby Airedale aerodrome site, now occupied by Esholt Sewage Works.*

Continue up the hill past St Leonard's Farm Park. Take the lane next right signed 'Bridleway and private road'. After 80 yards, turn left onto the path leading up to the steps and gate, meeting a path running from the car park.

Turn right. Follow the woodland path over the bridges and winding through the trees. By the stone wall there is a crossing of paths. Continue straight ahead, gradually ascending. At the next wall the path forks; take the right fork. At the next path junction at the apex of a bend, turn right. The path descends a little before bending left to follow a stream up a narrow valley in the woods. Where the path splits by a gate and bridge, keep left following the left bank of the stream, staying on the main path as you ascend.

At the next junction of paths, turn right. Go over the footbridge. Turn left to go up to the gate and stile, to meet a wider path. Turn left under the railway bridge. Follow the path up as it narrows and becomes stonier. The path ends at a street with modern housing. Turn left. Where the road bends off to the right, continue straight ahead along the track.

Primrose, wood sorrel and golden saxifrage are perennial species found in woodland, hedgerows and meadows.

Follow the track and, just before the main road, turn off right down Hawkhill Avenue. At the end, cross the main road with care to go down Victoria Road opposite. Follow Victoria Road until it emerges at the crossroads in the centre of Guiseley. Cross straight over and turn left down the cobbled road for the railway station on the right.

Guiseley is thought to have had its origins during the Saxon period, although a Stone Age axe and a Bronze Age urn have been found in the area. The settlement is assumed to have started in the Guiseley Wells area and been based on farming. In the eighteenth century the woollen industry expanded, beginning as a small-scale cottage industry, but by the Victorian era the stagecoaches, mills and railway arrived, fuelling expansion of the town. Until very recently, Guiseley had some notable manufacturing sites such as the Crompton Parkinson works as well as the Silver Cross pram factory. The largest fish and chip shop in the world, Harry Ramsden's, started business at nearby White Cross, once the terminus of the tram service from Leeds.

Airedale's green heart

Distance: 5 miles (8 km). Time: 2 hours.
Start: Apperley, the old stone bridge, grid ref 195380.
Parking: street parking on Apperley Road, near the George & Dragon.
Terrain: mostly level walking on riverside paths and canal towpath.
Refreshments/facilities: pubs and café in Apperley Bridge, pub in Calverley
on canalside; no public toilets.
Public transport: Bus 747 between Bradford and Leeds-Bradford Airport
serves Apperley Bridge; from Leeds, Shipley or Keighley, catch Bus 760 to
Greengates traffic lights and walk down to Apperley Bridge (half mile).
Map: Ordnance Survey Explorer 288.

Though this walk is on the outskirts of the cities of Leeds and Bradford, it enjoys part of an unspoiled green corridor of countryside shared by the River Aire, Leeds-Liverpool Canal and Leeds-Skipton railway line, along river and canal side, through woods and farmland, squeezed between old industry, busy outlying suburbs and ancient settlements of both cities.

The old stone-arch bridge over the River Aire at Apperley at the start of the walk was for many years in the days of stagecoaches the main crossing of the river between Harrogate and Bradford. Two fine coaching inns, the Stansfield Arms and George & Dragon, survive; the latter has the trunk of an ancient oak tree in the middle of the inn.

From the old bridge by the George Inn, make your way along Apperley Road to the main A658 Harrogate Road. Cross this busy and dangerous road at the lights of the toucan crossing. Turn left to cross the bridge, past Rawdon Meadow playing fields. Turn right into the entrance of Woodhouse Grove School (196380). Immediately to the right of the main school drive and security gate, a narrow path, enclosed between fence and trees, leads by sports grounds, before turning right after 200 yards to follow the enclosed way past rugby fields to the riverside. There are views across to Woodhouse Grove School from here.

Woodhouse Grove, a well-known independent educational establishment, has a long history, being originally founded in 1812 as a school for the sons of Methodist ministers. Charlotte Brontë was a governess in Upperwood House, a private residence which once occupied what is now part of the school site.

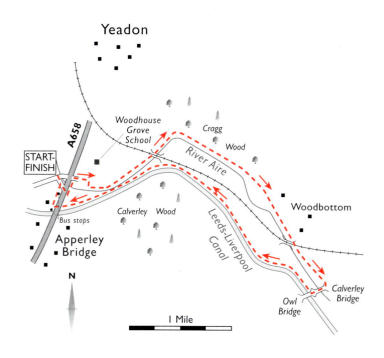

Turn left at the riverside, noting the council warnings to avoid this path at rare times of flood — though the path can be overgrown and muddy on any occasion. The path, narrow but well defined, follows the River Aire closely; the river flows quite strong and deep at this point, lined by old willows. Head under the Leeds-Skipton electrified railway line. Path and river eventually curve round into a steep gorge below Cragg Wood. Beyond here the path emerges at a track by a small house. Turn right here. Follow the tarmac track along a stone wall above water treatment works, with rural farmland belonging to Woodbottom Farm on the hillside above.

Approximately 400 yards from the junction (215378) where the track narrows to a path and bears left, there is another fork. Take the narrower path that bears right, down towards the riverside, between trees, soon going alongside the wire fence that marks the former Sandoz factory site. Continue to the next stone railway bridge. Go under an atmospheric narrow pedestrian tunnel under first a stone and then an iron bridge — a relic of the days when four railway tracks came into Leeds along the Aire Valley.

Follow the riverside until it meets the corner of Calverley Lane (222370). Do not take the path straight ahead, but turn sharp right down steps towards the picnic site. This leads onto the old cobbled packhorse bridge over the River Aire — the original Calverley Bridge. At the far side, keep straight ahead up steps. This leads onto a cobbled road up to the towpath of the Leeds-Liverpool Canal near Owl Bridge. (The Railway Inn is some 150 yards to the left.) Turn right along the towpath and continue along it for two miles (3 km).

This is surely one the most beautiful stretches of the 127-mile (203 km) canal. It is easy, level walking, past attractive fields and woods, parallel to the railway line above green fields, with the shallow river floodplain below.

Marsh marigolds and water avens, commonly seen on damp grassland.

Pass Lodge Bridge and go below Lodge Wood, the canal gradually curving to rejoin the river as you approach Apperley Bridge. Close to Apperley, pass a small farm on the right. Go under an iron bridge (no 214B).

You reach the next, larger road bridge (no 214A) carrying the main A658 Harrogate Road. If you are catching the Bradford bus, take the steps before this bridge and turn right to the bus stop. Otherwise go under the bridge to turn immediately right where a ramp leads you safely onto the pavement at the far side of the A658 by the Bridge Café. Keep ahead and turn first left for the George & Dragon and parked cars.